The John 10:10 Economic Worldview

A Life-Changing Paradigm Shift
in How You "See" the Kingdom of God

Doug Tjaden

ISBN 9798251705188

Printed in the United States of America

Released June 10, 2026

"The thief comes only to steal and kill and destroy; I came that you may have life, and have it abundantly."
Jesus ~ 29 A.D.

I didn't anticipate that when Jesus spoke those words, they held the key to understanding the global economic and monetary systems. Doug

Contents

Introduction

Most people sense it. Something is fundamentally broken in the global economic system. The results are all around us. Wealth concentrates at the top while poverty deepens at the bottom. Local communities hollow out as small businesses disappear and families struggle under mounting debt. Churches, though filled with sincere believers, often carry the same financial anxieties and consumption patterns that characterize the secular world around them. Creation groans under the weight of gross exploitation and mismanagement.[1] We are told that "it's just the way it is in a fallen world." But what if it was never meant to be this way? More importantly, *what if it doesn't have to remain this way?*

The struggle we face today, to live the abundant life spoken of by Jesus, is not merely the result of politicians and central bankers failing to manage a highly complex and deeply flawed global economy. The challenges are much more than structural. They are deeply spiritual—the result of humanity abandoning a brilliant economic design that God embedded into Creation. One that defined how He intended His image-bearers to create, steward, and exchange value, and to clearly understand the ultimate purpose for doing so. To build His Kingdom on earth.

[1] Romans 8:22

Restoring God's economic design and living the abundant life *is* possible today. However, it is not going to happen without a massive paradigm shift that re-defines the economic worldview embraced by followers of Jesus. The first and most painful step for many people will be defining value, wealth, abundance, and prosperity *as Jesus would.* And if biblical and secular history have taught us one thing, when a culture becomes comfortable with an abundance of "stuff," it becomes very difficult, if not impossible, to re-define those terms.

Fortunately, (or unfortunately, depending on your point of view), God has given us a point-in-time opportunity, that comes along once every few generations, to restore the definition of those terms. Then, to live life according to those definitions.

We have this opportunity now because we are entering a historically reliable, cyclical "reset" of the flawed economic and monetary systems designed by man. In the pages of this book, you will learn how stunningly regular such resets have been and why we are at this point once again.

With that said, it is one thing to know the history and "the why" it is happening. It is quite another to be positioned to influence the systems that will be produced by such a reset. With one or two exceptions, God's people have never been in such a position. Not because they have been forcefully excluded, but because they have not been equipped with a proper economic worldview to make any meaningful argument for the restoration of God's original design.

I believe God is asking us to change that.

To do so we must fully understand *what* He wants to accomplish, *why* He wants to do so at this time in history, and *how* He wants to bring it about. Basic biblical doctrine is a good place to start. We must acknowledge that we are in a real war between two "kingdoms" on earth.[2]

I have understood the theology behind that statement intellectually for decades. However, shortly after the year 2000, God began to take me on a journey that would allow me to understand the spiritual and practical reality of the "wartime economy" that every generation since the Garden of Eden has had no choice but to participate in. As I considered where to begin my study, I landed on a logical starting point. What does the Bible say about money? After all, there is plenty of material on that subject. While useful, it did not direct my focus to where God wanted. Instead, He kept directing my attention to a verse that, on the surface, seemed to have nothing to do with economics.

"The enemy came to steal, kill, and destroy; I came that you may have life, and have it abundantly."

As I prayed into what God wanted to reveal in this verse, Holy Spirit broke through. The stark contrast Jesus expressed in this single verse pointed directly to the "kings" engaged in the war between the two kingdoms. Satan and Himself. As God led me to tug

---

[2] Ephesians 6:12, Matthew 12:25-28, 1 John 5:19, et. al.

on the threads on each side of that verse (steal, kill, and destroy/abundant life), it proved to be a surprisingly concise summary of the motives, methods, and objectives of the two adversaries.

Jesus' motive was clear. In the beginning, Creation was brought into being through Him and by Him and for Him.[3] The Father then commanded humanity to "be fruitful and multiply and subdue the earth,"[4] effectively establishing His Kingdom throughout the earth. Satan had other plans. He aspired to "be like the Most High."[5] In Hebrew, that means to usurp the position, purpose and person of God. By extension that means he intends to establish *his* as the dominant kingdom on earth.

These two objectives are, of course, diametrically opposed. So, my questions became:

1) What does Scripture and history say about how each has waged this "economic" war?

2) What does Scripture and history say about who is winning the economic war?

3) What consequences have been experienced by humanity as this war has been waged throughout history?

4) What does all of this teach us about God's desired outcome as we experience another economic "reset?"

---

[3] Colossians 1:15-17, Hebrews 1:1-3b
[4] Genesis 1:28
[5] Isaiah 14:13-14

What follows in this book is a Holy Spirit revealed, real-life story told by Scripture that answers these questions and more. It is a summary of a three-book series, with nearly 600 pages and hundreds of footnotes, that I wrote over a five-year period.

I Came to Give – Understanding the Great Reset and the Coming Age of Abundance is the first book in the series. It is the story of God's original intention for His people to adopt His economic principles as the foundation upon which His Kingdom would be manifested on earth. It tells of Satan's desire for his own kingdom, which led him to replace God's economic principles with his own. It then traces the economic battle between these two kingdoms and its impact on humanity from the Garden of Eden to the present day.

The second book, *My Ways – A New Economic Worldview for the 21st Century Ekklesia*, is an in-depth exploration of the differences in God's economic principles and man's. It also emphasizes the importance of living out God's "economic worldview" today, beginning in our homes and extending to our local communities. It concludes with a practical framework to help local communities begin to adopt God's principles.

The final book in the series, *Cultivate and Keep – An Economic Foundation for the Great Restoration*, connects all of this by revealing a covenant between God, Jesus, humanity, and Creation. The purpose is to ensure that the parties remain connected relationally as humanity serves and protects Creation as the foundation of all economic activity on earth. It then explores the failure to uphold the covenant and the consequences. Finally, it calls us to restore the covenant, and with it, the starting point for a Kingdom-centered economic system.

What you read will likely be new to you. Not because I performed deep scholarship on the biblical text, but because I studied Scripture *through the lens of what the biblical writers intended to communicate to their contemporaries*—not an English-speaking American reading an English translation of the text thousands of years later.

This is of utmost importance. The only way to accurately transfer the intended meaning of the biblical writers, across time and culture, is by reading the Bible in its proper context. Application of this context is what revealed that there *is* a John 10:10 economic worldview contained in the pages of Scripture, and understanding it will have enormous implications for you, your church, your family, your community, and your nation in the coming years.

I wrote this consolidated book for one reason. The truths that God revealed in those three books need to be accessible to those who do not have the time or interest (at least not yet) to digest six-hundred pages of theological and historical economic "meat." This consolidated book is more lightly footnoted. However, it is my expectation that after reading this book, many of you will want to sit down and digest the meat and understand the full reality of what is ahead of us.

That is, a once in a multi-generation opportunity to begin the process of restoring an economic system that will enable us to create, steward, and distribute value across the earth as God intended. A system that will enable the body of Christ and the neighbors we love to finally enjoy the abundant life that Jesus came to give.

The Gospel as the Foundation

Everything in my books is anchored in Christ-centered theology. As such, I need to set the context from which I approach this thing we call "economics." It begins with establishing the gospel upon which this, and my other books, rest.

In the Western evangelical church, the gospel of salvation has been the focal point for decades—to the point of downplaying or even excluding the very gospel preached almost exclusively by Jesus during His ministry—the gospel of the Kingdom. Therefore, I cannot assume that every reader has been exposed to Kingdom theology. Certainly, the subject is much deeper than I can possibly cover here. As such, I will make a few observations that highlight what Scripture, and Jesus Himself, emphasized in His teachings and ministry.

A primary message of John the Baptist was that Jesus' arrival meant the Kingdom of God was "at hand." He called the people to prepare the way for the coming Lord and *King*.[6] When he was imprisoned and subsequently sent his disciples to ask Jesus if He was

---

[6] Matthew 3:1-3

the coming *Messiah King (not savior)*, Jesus told them to report that what He had declared in a synagogue in Nazareth (Luke 4) was happening in real time. It was evidence that the King had arrived and His Kingdom was indeed "at hand."

Central to the thesis of a Kingdom-centered economic worldview is the fact that Jesus is directly referenced as Savior less than twenty times in the New Testament. However, He is referenced as King approximately one hundred times, and Lord over five hundred times.

The Greek word for "king" is *basileus*, and it means "leader of the people, prince, commander, lord of the land, king." The Greek word for "lord" is *kyrios*, and it means "he to whom a person or thing belongs, about which he has the power of deciding; master, lord, the possessor and disposer of a thing, *the owner*." *Basilius*/king conveys leadership. *Kyrios*/lord conveys *ownership*. Three times in the New Testament Scripture also tells us that Jesus is "King of kings" and "Lord of lords."[7]

Scripture clearly tells us that Jesus is "Leader of all who lead," and "Owner of all that others claim to own." This has profound theological implications, not just for understanding the gospel of the Kingdom, but also for how God's Kingdom is to be perceived and managed on earth. This, in turn, directly ties to the practical and spiritual economic system that must be in place to serve His Kingdom.

---

7 1 Timothy 6:15, Revelation 17:14, 19:16

Redefining "Economics"

You may already be tired of reading the word "economics." Most people view the subject as boring at best, and confusing at worst. I get it. However, this book is different. That is because the Lord led me to examine the subject through the lens of what is required to prevail in economic warfare, and to accomplish our mandate to build God's Kingdom on earth as it is in heaven.[8] Therefore, to helpg you see this John 10:10 economic worldview, I redefine "economics" as:

> *"God's image bearers working together with Him, according to His principles and ways, to serve and protect Creation as we engage in trade that creates, secures, and deploys assets to build the Kingdom of God on earth while protecting and nurturing human dignity and identity."*

This definition lays aside boring traditional economic teaching, which focuses on charts, graphs, formulas, and sterile numeric monetary metrics such as ROI and GDP. It allows us to look with fresh eyes at key concepts through a principle-based lens and redefine terms like prosperity and wealth in spiritual and relational terms rather than material, transactional, and monetary terms.

This approach reveals a consistent, biblical, historically validated narrative of how God intended

---

[8] Matthew 6:10

His people to create, store, and deploy resources to build His Kingdom on earth (the abundant life). It also exposes how far we have drifted from His ways (leading to theft, death, and destruction), and why course correcting matters more today than perhaps at any point in history.

Be aware that at times I may use "economic" language in places that seem strange, or even inappropriate. I make no apologies for that. This book is about seeing the truth of the profound impact every form of "trade" has on human beings, individually and collectively, as we engage in the economic war being waged between the two kingdoms.

The Encounter That Made This All Real

I have studied money and economics since the turn of the century. Every time I study their history, I get angry. And sad. And angry again. When secular history books deal with the failure of economic and monetary systems, they present it through sterile academic language—dates and statistics showing how much GDP fell and how long it took to recover, and blah, blah, blah. Productivity metrics and how much "stuff" is being built, or not built, completely miss the heart of God. He is much more concerned with economic systems that build and protect the identity of human beings.

During those years of study, I began to learn about the immense human suffering brought about by man's economic and monetary systems. Although heartbreaking, I did not "feel" the pain from humanity's suffering in the same way that God does. Then, in 2007, God gave me a personal encounter that brought the reality of this suffering directly in front of me in a way that changed me forever.

My wife and I made a trip to Guatemala City with our three daughters to bring home the first of our two adopted sons. While we were there, we traveled to Antigua, a tourist town not far from the city. As we rode the bus along winding roads, I noticed that the people became poorer as the landscape became more rural.

Children with dirty and tattered clothes tended chickens or pigs in makeshift pens. A few adults were carrying water. Some just sat on the dirt floors of their huts in their own tattered clothes, watching as another tourist bus filled with Americans passed by. As a dutiful Christian, I took note of their plight and said a silent prayer on their behalf.

When we reached Antigua, the city came alive again. Shops full of trinkets and vibrantly colored clothes lined the streets. Tourists were busy negotiating with the locals. All this activity made the images I had seen on the bus fade into the background. My attention shifted back to my family and the fun of exploring this quaint little town.

On the way to one of the historical sites, I was approached in the street by a girl about ten years old. She was carrying a worn wicker basket of trinkets that she hoped I would buy. I smiled and noted that she was around the same age as my oldest daughter. She even looked a little like her, with dark hair, dark skin, and dark eyes. It was her eyes that caught my attention. I will never forget them. It was the first time in my life that I looked into a child's eyes and saw…nothing.

Usually, there is a glint of light or brightness in a child's eyes that holds the promise of life and a future. Not with this little girl. There was an emptiness in her eyes that is hard to describe. At that moment, it hit me—this precious little girl spent her days on the streets hustling strangers for *money*. I shuddered to think about what she may have been required to sell to other strangers by night.

The thought crushed me. Tears filled my eyes as I walked away from that beautiful child, created in the image of God. He knit both her and my daughter together in their mother's wombs. They were both given special gifts and talents. Both had hopes and dreams, and God's heart was that both would someday join their families in building His Kingdom.

Yet, their lives could not have been more different. That little girl's identity was stolen from her. She didn't give it up willingly. And a major reason for that theft is an economic system, designed by Satan himself to steal, kill, and destroy that little girl's life. Her suffering, along with countless millions of others, will continue to serve as motivation for me to keep pursuing the restoration of God's economic principles in our homes, churches, communities, and nations for the rest of my natural life.

My friend, given the present state of the world's economic and monetary systems, it is more important than ever that the church – the ekklesia – the body of

Christ – followers of Jesus – whatever you want to call us, get a firm grasp on economic reality and enter into a strategic plan to proactively respond to what is unfolding before us. Whatever comes from my efforts, I am doing this for my children, grandchildren, that little girl, and most of all, for the sake of our King, Jesus Christ.

Chapter 1
In the Beginning...

"Your Kingdom Come, your will be done on earth as it is in heaven."
Matthew 6:10

Before the first seed spouted, before He created man, God envisioned a Kingdom. He would fill it with His human family, and it would operate according to the laws of physics and a set of principles that He would weave into the very fabric of Creation. He would bring it into existence by and through the one it was created for—Jesus.[9] The principles would express the trinity's own character—reflections of how all things natural and supernatural would be governed.

With this in mind, I would like you to entertain a thought experiment. Please take the time to go through this exercise, because it sets important context for how God originally intended humanity to interact with one another in the world that He was about to create.

To begin, imagine that you are one of the first two members of this new family, Adam or Eve. You are in the Garden having daily face-to-face conversations with the Creator of everything you see. As you develop

---

[9] John 1:1-5; Colossians 1:16-17; Hebrews 1:3a

your relationship with God, three things quickly become evident.

First, He loves you. Second, He has created you to love as well. There is a reciprocal nature of this thing called love that creates an intimate bond between you and God and between you and your spouse that is impossible to describe. You sense that love is the center of all things; however, it is not yet clear exactly what "all things" includes. Finally, you sense the power of relationship. Within the Trinity, the Father creates,[10] the Son sustains,[11] and the Holy Spirit teaches and guides.[12] This relationship models how God intends humanity to work together.

Next, you realize that you were created for a purpose that is larger than you can imagine.[13] It is a "project" that begins with you and your spouse in a tiny garden on a very big earth. Your garden may be small, but it is incredible. God has filled it with an abundance of plants, animals, and creeping creatures. As you tend to the garden, you discover a few important things about Creation.

First, there is an abundance of *everything*.[14] Second, it all belongs to God,[15] and you are to manage it according to His will. Third, the depth of love between you and God has created an unshakable bond of trust. Not only do you trust Him without question,

---

[10] Genesis 1:1
[11] John 1:1-3
[12] John 16:13
[13] Genesis 1:28
[14] Genesis 1:11,12,20-25
[15] Psalms 50:10-12

but He also has entrusted *you* to manage His Creation[16] as part of a "grand building project."

As you learn the details of this project it seems almost too good to be true. He informs you that you and all your descendants will become creators just like Him. You will create structures to live in, transportation systems, and tools to harvest the abundance Creation produces for you. He tells you that, over time, you may also create things that will enable you to communicate with humans all over the earth (why would we need that?).

You stand in awe as God tells you that soon you will produce other humans to love and build relationships with. He reveals more of His vision for what He means by "be fruitful and multiply and subdue the earth." God explains to you that He will give each human a unique set of talents[17] that will manifest the very essence of Him on earth. He will show you all how to use those talents, along with the design of Creation's ecosystems, to bring this magnificent project to life and extend it throughout the planet that you are just beginning to explore.

With excitement and full trust in your Creator, you begin. At first, progress is slow. However, time is of no concern. There is no deadline. Every day, you and your family listen to God's instructions, learn, and build. The next day, you do it all over again. Each day brings fresh revelation. As you steward God's

---

[16] Matthew 25:14-30, John 3:27, 1 Corinthians 9:17, et. al.

[17] Romans 12:6-8, 1 Peter 4:10, Philippians 2:10

abundant natural resources,[18] the "project" begins to take shape.

Now, fast forward about three hundred years. Imagine that you and your spouse have about forty children (do not forget, women—no pain in childbirth!). Multiple generations have produced several thousand human beings. They each bear God's image, have their own unique set of gifts and talents, and have the same intimate relationship with the Creator as you.

The pace at which the project expands quickens. You and your descendants have learned how to create metal alloys and compounds that we have yet to discover today. We can scarcely imagine what you have built! What you see take shape around you is an extension of the creativity of God Himself!

Your relationship with Creation transcends mere stewardship of its abundant natural resources. You understand and seamlessly incorporate the perfect design of natural ecosystems into the systems, structures, and machines that you build. And they work perfectly! Every system is perfect in its design. Nothing goes to waste. And because there is no law of entropy (remember, this is before the fall), you build and move on to the next project. It all has a purpose, and it works together. It is awesome! And wonderful!

As the project unfolds, you gain a better understanding of God's ultimate vision for His project. It consists of communities of human beings spending

---

[18] Genesis 1:11-25

long periods of time developing deep relationships. His human family naturally supports and encourages each other to develop the gifts and talents that God placed in them. They plan. They build. They worship. They love their neighbors deeply.

The material world increasingly reflects the same splendor and glory found in heaven.[19] The relationships you have with your fellow image-bearers, God, and His council[20] are nothing short of fantastic! Leaders operate from the posture of servanthood. They recognize their profound responsibility to advance the project by first nurturing each person's relationship with God. They understand that doing so empowers each person to fully manifest the gifting that He placed within them.

The God-ordained family becomes the center of community health and is the foundation of the "economic engine" that will complete the project.[21] The prevailing "culture" on the entire earth is one where every person is content with having their basic material needs—food, clothing, and shelter[22]—met. Natural resources are put to their highest and best use to maximize humanity's expression of the fruits of the Spirit as they fellowship with God and other image-bearers. Loving your neighbor is as natural as loving yourself and God.[23] You discover that this love also includes loving Creation.

---

[19] John 6:10
[20] Psalm 82:1, Deuteronomy 32:8-9, 1 Kings 22:19–23, et. al.
[21] Genesis 12:3
[22] Matthew 6:25-34, Philippians 4:11-12
[23] Matthew 22:37-39

With no opposition, over time God's family advances the project at an exponential rate. You do not know when, but at some point, the project will be complete. The earth will be subdued! As this time rapidly approaches, a question on everyone's mind is, "What's next, God?!?"

Back to Reality

As we all know, this thought experiment is not how history played out. However, it is a logical approximation of how God *desired* history to unfold. So why would we think that His desire for humanity to undertake this grand building project—to build His Kingdom on earth—has changed, even within the constraints of sin and entropy thwarting its progress? The answer is, *it hasn't.*

That realization kept me in the first three chapters of Genesis. As I examined the Creation narrative and the Fall in detail, God revealed a set of five non-negotiable economic principles that would be required to accomplish the mandate He gave humanity—a mandate, by the way, that He not only has never revoked, but He restated it to Noah after the Great Flood.[24]

These principles formed the foundation of everything written in my books. Understanding them *in their proper biblical and historical context* is critical. They draw a clear line of separation between a true biblical economic worldview and the one held by most followers of Jesus today which, unfortunately,

[24] Genesis 9:1-17

is nothing more than “the economic traditions of men.”[25] The five principles are:

Cooperation. Adam and Eve did not work in isolation. They worked closely with God, Jesus, Creation, and each other. Each human contributes to the grand building project through reciprocal, synergistic relationships.

Stewardship. Nothing belongs to humanity by right of “ownership.” Everything belongs to God.[26] He entrusts it to our care to do His will for the sake of our King and His Kingdom.

Abundance. Creation lacks nothing. God's genius concept of “seed” as the means of reproduction empowers it to produce, in perpetuity, more than enough for the needs of every living creature, including and especially humanity.

Identity as God’s image bearers. God created humans in His image[27] with skills and gifts that enable us to perform functions like Him. This includes the ability to create and govern like Him on earth to manifest His Kingdom here.

Sustainability. God designed Creation with the foreknowledge that His created creatures would rebel. The design is so incredible that the earth’s ecosystems are resilient enough to regenerate after something as catastrophic as a global flood.

---

[25] Mark 7:9-13
[26] Psalm 24:1
[27] Genesis 1:27

When designed into an economic system, these five principles form an integrated, dynamic "ecosystem" that enables humanity to flourish. You will see this reality demonstrated as you read further. First, however, I need to take a moment and establish a key component of God's economic plan for humanity. Like the thought experiment, it provides important context for what you will read in the remainder of the book.

The Covenant

A biblical hermeneutic that I hold closely is the Law of First Mention. This states that the closer a word, concept, or principle can be tied to its first appearance—ideally in or near the act of Creation—the more clearly it reveals God's heart and original intentions for humanity. When I applied this to the creation narrative, it led me to the correct chronological starting point, which is not the first chapter of Genesis, but rather the first chapter of John.

> "In the beginning was the Word, and the Word was with God, and the Word was God. He was in the beginning with God. All things came into being through Him, and apart from Him nothing came into being that has come into being. In Him was life, and the life was the Light of men. The Light shines in the darkness, and the darkness did not comprehend it."
> John 1:1-5

These verses provide critical context for the creation narrative in Genesis 1 and 2. They also help us interpret other New Testament passages that reveal Jesus' role in the act of creation. Let's look at three of them.

> "[Jesus] is the image of the invisible God, the firstborn of all creation. For by Him all things were created, both in the heavens and on earth, visible and invisible, whether thrones or dominions or rulers or authorities—all things have been created through Him and for Him. He is before all things, and in Him all things hold together."
> Colossians 1:15-17

> "God, after He spoke long ago to the fathers in the prophets in many portions and in many ways, in these last days has spoken to us in His Son, whom He appointed heir of all things, through whom also He made the world. And He is the radiance of His glory and the exact representation of His nature, and upholds all things by the word of His power."
> Hebrews 1:1-3a

There is a lot packed into these verses that is often overlooked on a casual reading. For example, building on John 1:1-5 and examining the Greek definition of several key words and phrases opens the door to a wonderful discovery. In all three passages, the word "through" in Greek is *dia*, which means "the channel of an act; because of; by occasion of, by reason of, for the sake of." In Colossians 1:17, the Greek word for "hold together" is *synistaō*, and it means "to place together, to set in the same place, to bring or band together." Finally, in Hebrews 1:3, the Greek words for "upholds," "all things," "word," and "power" are *pherō, pas, rhēma, and dynamos*. They mean to bring forward and bear up everything through the power residing in a thing by virtue of its nature, using a spoken word. Now let's look at the final verse. It's a statement Jesus made in the book of Revelation:

> "The Amen, the faithful and true Witness, the Beginning of the creation of God…"
> Revelation 3:14

Jesus identifies Himself as "the Beginning of the creation of God." That is quite a claim. Yet the Greek word for "Beginning" is *archē* and it means "the person or thing that commences, the first person or thing in a series, the leader that by which anything begins to be, the origin, *the active cause*." The proceeding verses support Jesus' claim. Combined they tell us that…

By the spoken Word of the Father, Creation came into existence through the Son. It exists for His sake and is held together physically and remains in existence today by virtue of who Jesus is and by the power of His Word.

Please read that again. God created a universe in which He strategically initiated intimate relationships between Himself, His Son, Creation, and humans, and Jesus is the centering point that holds them all together. When I studied the first two chapters of Genesis with this important context in view *and in chronological order,* Scripture revealed how intimate these relationships are, and how they form the foundation of God's economy. It began with God stating His desire to create a human family.

"Then God said, 'Let Us make man in Our image, according to Our likeness;"
Genesis 1:26a

To continue chronologically, we must go to Genesis 2.

"Then the LORD God formed man of dust from the ground, and breathed into his nostrils the breath of life; and man became a living being."
Genesis 2:7

We know that God created man from the elements already placed into Creation. However, did you consider that the Father (the breath of life), the earthly, natural world (Creation), and the Son (through whom it occurs and is held together by the power of His Word) all participated in creating humans? The relational bond formed with each could not get any more intimate than that!

Verses that chronologically precede and follow the creation of man identify a critical responsibility that was given to humans, as members of this new intimate relational bond. Interestingly, the verse proceeding it begins with God identifying a problem.

"Now no shrub of the field was yet in the earth, and no plant of the field had yet sprouted, for the LORD God had not sent rain upon the earth, and there was no man to cultivate the ground."
Genesis 2:5

And the verse following it describes how God intended to solve the problem.

"Then the LORD God took the man and
put him into the garden of Eden to
cultivate it and keep it."
Genesis 2:15

Combined, these verses reveal humanity's primary responsibility in our relationship with Creation. To fully understand it we must examine the Hebrew text.

The word for "cultivate" is *âḇar*. It is used 290 times in Scripture, and its primary root means "to serve." It is also used several times in the context of "worshipper." The Hebrew word for "keep" is *šâmar*, meaning to "guard, observe, give heed, have charge of, keep watch and ward, protect, save life."

God needed stewards to serve and nurture Creation so that it could sustainably produce in abundance. He needed them to protect it as well. After all, God knew about the one who would soon seek to steal, kill, and destroy all that He had created, and He knew *how* he planned to do it. Therefore, God placed an important restriction on Adam's stewardship mandate.

"The LORD God commanded the man, saying,
"From any tree of the garden you may eat
freely; but from the tree of the knowledge of
good and evil you shall not eat, for in the day
that you eat from it you will surely die."
Genesis 2:16-17

God was clear. Of all My Creation, pay particular attention to "protect" this tree. Do not eat from it. If you fail, it will unleash consequences beyond what you can imagine. Then God provided Creation with the final, beautiful piece that enabled humanity to fulfill its intended purpose.

When God created Eve by taking her out of Adam's body, it further demonstrated His commitment to connect man, woman, Creation, and Jesus with Himself in the most intimate possible way physically and spiritually. When He was finished God declared His Creation was "very good."

God had not only established a human family. He also established a de facto covenant between the parties in this new relational compact. The covenant is necessary for humanity to generate the resources to fulfill the mandate of Genesis 1:28—to be fruitful, multiply and establish His Kingdom throughout the earth.

I must acknowledge that using the word "covenant" is a serious claim with major implications. Therefore, let me take a moment and establish why what I just described qualifies as a covenant. Bible scholars generally agree that there is a "covenantal framework" in Scripture that contains covenants, both declared and undeclared, by God. Those that are undeclared are identified by several key characteristics.

1. *Covenantal Connection*: The actions in the undeclared covenant are intimately linked with declared covenants. For example, the Feast of

Unleavened Bread is not directly named by God as a covenant. However, it is directly linked to the Passover. The Passover is a key moment in God's covenant with Abraham and his descendants, marking their deliverance and their subsequent covenantal commitment to God.

2. *Permanent Ordinance*: The Feast of Unleavened Bread is commanded as a permanent ordinance, to be observed from generation to generation. This perpetual nature aligns with the concept of covenant, which involves ongoing obligations and memorials.
3. *Covenantal Obedience*: Upholding or failing to uphold a covenant has serious consequences that reach throughout the generations.
4. *Symbolic Significance*: Upholding the terms of the covenant becomes a symbol in other teachings.

A familiar example of a covenant that we all recognize, that is not named specifically in Scripture, is marriage. We refer to it as a covenant, because the defining characteristics of a covenant are inherently present in this relationship between a man and woman.

Similarly, these characteristics are plainly evident in the relationships God established between Himself, Jesus, Creation, and humanity during the act of creation. The intimate and perpetual nature of these relationships, along with the requirement for each party to fulfill specific responsibilities for the covenant to be enforceable, supports a covenantal view. These responsibilities are clearly defined:

1. *God* provides an incredible, diverse natural ecosystem for humanity.
2. *Jesus* upholds and sustains this ecosystem by the power of His word.
3. *Humanity* is to cultivate and keep the ecosystem—to serve and protect it.
4. *Creation* will "give up its strength"[28] to yield an abundance of the human and natural resources necessary to build the Kingdom of God on earth.

God established this early Covenant in part because nurturing the ground, planting seeds, and watching them produce abundant life-sustaining food is nothing short of a miracle. From the beginning of time, He intended that cultivating and keeping the earth would be a primary centering point for every human being to relate to Him, His Son, Creation, and our neighbors.

In fact, providing life-giving sustenance to our fellow human beings was meant to be one of the most honored positions anyone could hold in His Kingdom. It seems obvious. Abundant nutritious food is a non-negotiable requirement for humanity to be fruitful,

---

[28] Genesis 4:12

multiply, and subdue the earth. Without it, there is no Kingdom!

This Covenant establishes that Creation is not merely the stage on which human economic activity is conducted. It is an economic partner with us, with its own critical role in the story of building God's Kingdom on earth. It defines both humanity's role and our *obligations* as we seek to fulfill the mandate given to us in Genesis 1:28. It is critical to understand this if we are to correct the errors in today's biblical economic worldview.

Chapter 2
The Rebel Who Changed It All

"...I will be like the Most High."
Isaiah 14:14 (NKJV)

In Genesis 3 we are introduced to an antagonist who is intent on thwarting God's plans. The origin of Satan's rebellion, as revealed in Ezekiel 27 and 28, is not merely his backstory. It reveals the profile of one skilled in the art of trade, and who set about to use those skills to acquire the resources needed to build a kingdom that would compete with God's to become the dominant kingdom on earth.

It is an uncontested fact that every kingdom requires real, practical resources to grow and expand its territory. With a second kingdom now vying for Creation's resources, the economic war had begun. Satan wanted resources to flow to his kingdom. He wanted power to concentrate under him. And that required humans to bear his image, rather than God's.

To accomplish this, Satan introduced principles that speak directly to fallen human nature. The rebellion in Genesis 3 records the moment these counterfeit principles entered the world. It will come as no surprise that they directly counter God's original five principles.

- Control and competition replaced cooperation.
- Ownership replaced stewardship.
- Scarcity replaced abundance.
- Identity theft replaced identity security.
- Fragility replaced sustainability.

The trinity, in its essence, demonstrates that love and trust are the bonds that hold relationships together. Therefore, Satan's strategy was to *separate* all parties to the Covenant by introducing two new spirits into the Garden of Eden—control and competition.

According to most teachings, Eve first sinned when she bit the fruit. However, God told Adam and Eve not to *touch* the fruit.[29] Thus, when Eve reached out and plucked the fruit from the tree, she took *control* of an item that God had forbade her to possess. In that moment, she broke the Covenant God established by turning her back on her responsibility to serve and protect Creation. Instead, she claimed *ownership* over the fruit, using it to fulfill *her* purposes, not God's. Stop and consider what that means.

When Satan convinced Eve to steal from God, it made her into a thief—for the very reason he became one—to "be like God."[30]

The consequences for each were strikingly similar. Satan was cast from heaven because he conducted theft in trade in the heavenly realm.

[29] Genesis 3:3
[30] Genesis 3:4,5

> "By the abundance of your trade
> You were internally filled with violence,
> And you sinned; Therefore I have cast you as profane From the mountain of God."
> Ezekiel 28:16

Eve and her spouse were cast from the Garden of Eden.

> "Then the LORD God said, "Behold, the man has become like one of Us, knowing good and evil; and now, he might stretch out his hand, and take also from the tree of life, and eat, and live forever"— therefore the LORD God sent him out from the garden of Eden…"
> Genesis 3:22-23a

Note that God was not only concerned that they would eat the fruit of the tree of life. He was also concerned they would "take" from it—and once again bear the image of the thief and steal the fruit. I trust you can now begin to see more clearly Satan's method of operation as it relates to gathering assets for his kingdom. *Steal* material goods, *kill* humanity spiritually, and *destroy* our relationship with God, Jesus, Creation, and other human beings.

Something else to note here is that God is consistent in administering justice. Similar sins produce consistent and related consequences. Keep this in mind as you read the remainder of this book as it supports key conclusions I draw in my book series and indicates a possible future that lies ahead of us.

When Adam and Eve realized what they had done, their first reaction was to hide from God. The intimacy of their relationship with Him had been compromised. They knew it, and they were terrified. In their fear, when confronted by God, the second of the two new spirits made its presence known—competition.

When Adam blamed Eve for giving him the fruit, the cooperative partnership between the parties of the Covenant gave way to self-serving *competition*. By instigating "the blame game" Adam was, in effect, attempting to shift the consequences of his sin to Eve. If God assigned fault to Eve alone, Adam would "win." As we know, God did not play the game.

Unfortunately for humanity though, the devastating consequences of the spirit of competition had only begun, and it did not just affect human beings. The ground was cursed[31]—not by God as an arbitrary punishment, but because of human sin. Fruitful plants and animals, designed and given to humanity as food,[32] would now have to compete with thorns and predators to survive. The earth's ability to produce in abundance carried no guarantee of success. As Adam and Eve and their family began to witness this firsthand, it gave rise to a fear of *scarcity*. This unfortunately caused them to engage in more *competition* and *control* as they began to believe there was no other means to obtain what they needed to survive.

[31] Genesis 3:17-19

[32] Genesis 1:29-30

Within one generation, this toxic economic environment caused Cain to take ultimate *control* over life itself. He murdered Abel over a perceived competitive loss to gain God's approval of their offerings. From that day forward, the spirits of control and competition expanded their role in the story of humanity. So much so that human civilization became organized around those who could best compete with others and control them to accumulate and claim ownership of resources for their personal benefit.

But this is just the beginning. We have only scratched the surface of the damage Satan's economic principles inflicted on humanity. His ultimate objective is to recruit human assets to build his kingdom by stealing, killing, and destroying their *identity*.

Contradicting God's command to avoid the tree of knowledge of good and evil was not just about following God's rules. It was Satan's challenge to the "*ruler*." He drew into question who God is and, by extension, if humanity should *really* desire to bear His image.

When Eve exchanged her identity as a bearer of God's image for Satan's image as a thief, it revealed a critical vulnerability in Satan's strategy. He cannot acquire resources to build his kingdom without first engaging in identity theft.

Unfortunately, Satan is very good at what he does. He knows that when human identity is separated from God, it creates a void that must be filled. In today's western world, we have been conditioned to fill this void with material goods and services that gratify our desires. The economic system that delivers these void-filling distractions is capitalism.

The Academic Pharisees that inhabit our education system convince us that capitalism is the "best economic system ever devised by man." However, we fail to acknowledge that, at its core, capitalism encourages humans to compete for ownership of resources and use them to please ourselves. When we do (which is painfully frequent) it makes us no less of a thief than Eve. Ultimately, this results in a spiral where we trade our dignity, our bodies, and often, ultimately, our souls to obtain more resources to fill the widening void between our identity as a thief and God's desired identity in Him.

This assertion is one to which I get some of the most intense disagreement. But as you will see later, (and it is most certainly documented in my book series) the results of capitalism have been catastrophic for humanity. A primary reason is that economic systems built on competition, ownership, and scarcity, (which by the way, are explicitly named in the definition of capitalism), will eventually become unsustainable.

Those at the top of the economic pyramid are incentivized to create efficient trading systems and supply chains that centralize control (and thus profits) in fewer and fewer hands. Simultaneously, as they become more efficient, they develop multiple "single points of failure." When one of those points breaks, it threatens the viability of the entire system and creates hardship for the people using it.

Now, apply this reality to our global economic system. We witnessed this during the Covid lockdowns. A more recent example is the closure of the Strait of Hormuz. In each case, the effects of disrupting single points of failure will produce repercussions that will last for years.

Fragile economic systems have failed throughout history with remarkable consistency. That is because fragility is not an accident or an unfortunate side effect. It is embedded in the structural design of systems built on principles that violate God's design.

The Tower of Babel: An Unexpected Example of Cooperation at Scale

Few stories reveal the power of God's Kingdom-building principles as clearly as the rebellion of the gentile nations at the Tower of Babel. It tells of a unified humanity, speaking one language, that decided to build a tower to the heavens—not to honor God, but to "make a name" for themselves. Not a "name" associated with bearing the image of God, but instead, one bearing the image of His enemy. God's response is remarkable:

> "The LORD said, 'Behold, they are one people, and they all have the same language. And this is what they began to do, and now nothing which they purpose to do will be impossible for them.'"
> Genesis 11:6

There is a profound economic truth contained in what God said in that verse:

The power of cooperative, unified human effort is unstoppable.

Sadly, Satan understands this better than followers of Jesus. His strategy is to steal, kill, and destroy human capacity to build God's kingdom while simultaneously imprinting people with his identity, thereby harnessing their ability to cooperate to build his kingdom. God stopped this at the Tower of Babel by confusing their language. This immediately cut off their communication lines and their ability to gather and deploy resources. It was a brilliant use of a basic warfare tactic that has been used throughout history.

We cannot miss the fact that by doing this, God also prohibited them from co-opting His principle of cooperation and using it against Him. They could no longer achieve their objectives, which would have devastated humanity. It should be noted that every human empire since Babel has been, in some measure, a continuation of the same objective—to build a kingdom that competes with God's.

This leads to a critical point. The kings of the earth will always design and implement economic systems that benefit their "kingdoms." That, however, does not mean that the ekklesia should accept their systems, including capitalism, as acceptable ways to manage resources within the Kingdom of God.

In fact, nowhere in Scripture will you find a command or law for *God's people* to compete with one another, nor any instance of a positive outcome when they do so. Instead, we must compete with *the principalities and powers* (Ephesians 6:10-12) behind socialism and capitalism by showing humanity *a better way,* as we adopt God's principles within His Kingdom. I spend a great deal of time addressing this in *My Ways*. Unfortunately, since the early church, followers of Jesus have struggled to do this. Why?

The Traditions of Men

In the process of researching Scripture and history when writing *I Came to Give*, it became clear that the Western church largely embraced capitalism. Not as a matter of intentional rebellion, but as a recurring pattern throughout Scripture. God's people have consistently adopted the culture and traditions of the secular nation-state they occupy. In my books, I develop the theological case made by Jesus that such "traditions of men" make "the word of God of no effect,"[33] and result in devastating consequences for humanity.

The 2002 BBC documentary, *The Century of the Self*,[34] which I reference in *I Came to Give*, is an example of how accepting the economic traditions of men during the twentieth century left the door wide open for the enemy to embed satanic manipulative practices into the fabric of Western economic systems. These practices have only been amplified in today's 24/7 online, social media-driven world.

---

[33] Mark 7:5-13

[34] https://www.youtube.com/watch?v=DnPmg0R1M04

When pastors and church leaders limit their teaching about economics to tithing, "debt is bad," and "money is neither good nor bad, all that matters it how you use it," they leave one of the most powerful systems in the world to the adversary. The result is a church culture where transformation is preached while attendees live in financial anxiety. Where abundance is proclaimed while people continue to operate under scarcity. And where followers of Jesus are called to work together while they remain siloed off in thousands of competing denominations.

This is the "spiritual inertia" that keeps Christians locked into patterns of thinking and behaving that are fundamentally incompatible with the economic principles of God's Kingdom. It is not due to malice. Rather, is the accumulated weight of generations of traditions of men making their way into a false economic worldview. That worldview then produces economic systems that make the word of God no effect, as it rewards those who conform to its principles and punish those who deviate from them. I believe it is time to break this spiritual inertia once and for all.

Chapter 3

Worldview, Trading Floors, and Breaking Spiritual Inertia

"For there was not a needy person among them,…"
Acts 4:34a

In *My Ways*, I press into the question of why Christians so consistently fail to apply God's economic principles, even when they intellectually affirm them. The answer, not surprisingly, lies at the level of worldview.

A worldview is not merely a set of beliefs. It is the invisible interpretive framework through which we perceive reality—the set of assumptions about the world that are so deeply embedded they feel like common sense rather than chosen perspectives. Our worldview shapes what we notice, what we dismiss, what possibilities we can imagine, and what constraints we accept as normative, appropriate, and immovable.

Most Western Christians operate with a profoundly bifurcated worldview—one that has deep historical roots in the separation of sacred and secular, spiritual and natural, eternal and temporal. This separation owes more to Greek philosophy than to Scripture. It has produced a church that accepts such tripe as "we have the best economic system ever devised by man," rather than considering if there is a better way—one devised by God.

This bifurcation is precisely what Satan needs to maintain his economic stronghold. As long as Christians believe that their Bible has nothing substantive to say about how they create, store, and deploy economic resources, they will continue to accept scarcity, competition, and ownership as economic facts rather than spiritual choices. In short, they will continue operating within Satan's system and assisting to build his kingdom rather than making the effort to adopt God's way of building His.

Reforming this worldview requires more than information. It requires a paradigm shift in how we see reality. My first book, *I Came to Give*, is derived from the single verse that ultimately gave way to the title of this book. By following the two threads (steal, kill, destroy/abundant life) throughout Scripture and economic history, God revealed that Scripture indeed contains a historically proven and theologically sound biblical economic worldview—a John 10:10 economic worldview.

This is why, in my books and video series, I begin, not with economic strategies, but with biblical vision: helping people see what God intended, so they can begin to move toward it. Scripture says, "You shall know the truth and the truth will set you free." Education is the first act of liberation. The transformation will begin when we recognize that there is no separation between the spiritual and the natural in God's economy. They are intimately intertwined. Understanding this will help us stop believing that trade is based on transactions and instead see that it is based on…

Relationships: The Force Multiplier of the Kingdom Economy

As we learned in chapter one, God's economy is fundamentally relational. It does not operate through isolated individuals maximizing personal gain. It operates through networks of trust, reciprocity, and shared purpose—what economists sometimes call "social capital," but what the Bible calls community.

The early church, described in Acts 2-4, is the most powerful historical demonstration of God's people putting His economic principles into action at a pivotal time in history.

> "And the congregation of those who believed were of one heart and soul; and not one of them claimed that anything belonging to him was his own, but all things were common property to them. And with great power the apostles were giving testimony to the resurrection of the Lord Jesus, and abundant grace was upon them all. For there was not a needy person among them, for all who were owners of land or houses would sell them and bring the proceeds of the sales and lay them at the apostles' feet, and they would be distributed to each as any had need."
> Acts 4:32-35

The contrast between the early church's stewardship of resources and that of the Romans was stark, even though the economic environment they lived in during the early first century was quite challenging. Few people realize that during Jesus' ministry, and for years after His resurrection, the Roman Empire experienced profound economic hardship, concluding with a full-blown financial crisis in 33 A.D. The economy had become based on extraction, tribute, taxation, slavery, and conquest—the fruit of control, competition, ownership, and scarcity. Wealth flowed upward to Rome and outward to the imperial armies. The poor stayed poor. The vulnerable had little to no safety net. In many cases people traded their dignity for survival.

In contrast, the early church practiced cooperation, stewardship, and an abundance mindset. They saw Jesus feed the five thousand with just a few loaves of bread and fishes. Thus, they gave freely to others as they had need. Relational exchange triumphed over marketplace transactions. Wealth was measured in the emotional, physical, and spiritual well-being of the community, not in the quantity of gold or silver coins in the treasury.

Today, when I suggest that managing church resources in this manner may produce similar results, many people, especially Christian business owners, become uncomfortable. They worked hard to "build my business" and they project socialism into the Acts 2-4 narrative (that is not there). They claim that I am suggesting socialism may be better than capitalism. Of course, that is not the case. However, most have a difficult time accepting that capitalism is also fatally flawed.

Their replies expose how deep the economic traditions of men, taught by the economic Pharisees that were hired by the kings of the earth, have been pushed into our worldview. They also reveal a major problem in the ability of followers of Jesus' to engage in discussions about economic principles today.

Logic and Reason

God expects His people to be ready to defend biblical principles in the public arena regarding matters important to His Kingdom.[35] Unfortunately, most followers of Jesus have little or no training in the laws of logic and reason. Critical thinking and intellectual curiosity have been set aside in favor of legalism, hyper-spirituality, or cultural assimilation. This phenomenon has caused the ekklesia to fail to consider that just because capitalism is the best economic system devised by man (I concede that point) does not mean it is the best *possible* system that can serve humanity.

In the study of logic, limiting options to an "either/or" proposition is a logical fallacy known as the "false dilemma." This is a tactic intentionally deployed in a debate to stop one's opponent from considering alternative arguments. From an economic perspective, because followers of Jesus have fallen for this fallacy, they believe they must choose between

---

[35] Isaiah 1:18, 1 Peter 3:15

socialism and capitalism, or worse yet, between socialism and the system we actually have today—corporatism.

This unholy alliance between the spirits of control and competition produces monopolistic multi-national corporations that "cooperate" with centralized governments to build an economic Tower of Babel where they sit as "gods" controlling the world's resources. Meanwhile, the world's citizens continue to argue over socialism vs. capitalism while the kings of the earth happily advance their agenda. For humanity, the consequences of this foolishness are staggering.

Unfortunately, without an economic worldview of their own, followers of Jesus will continue to argue for capitalism. As a result, unless corrected, the spirits of control and competition, along with Satan's principles of ownership, scarcity, identity theft, and fragility will remain in control of the world's economic and monetary systems. This is the reason I am dedicated to reforming the church's biblical economic worldview. Doing so will destroy the grip this logical fallacy has on the church, freeing us to pursue a new, albeit radical, alternative, based on God's principles and ways.

A Legal Framework for Trading Activity

Along with applying the laws of logic and reason, a biblical economic worldview must also include an understanding of the legal framework, contained in God's law, regarding the exchange of value. The legal question is important because it directly relates to the *biblical legality of any trade made by followers of Jesus'*. This carries massive implications in the spiritual world and in the Kingdom of God. What follows will give you a grid through which to process some of those implications.

Legal trades are binding. Illegal trades are not binding, and they can be reversed in a court with the proper jurisdiction. I will have more to say about this in the next chapter. For now, know that we can analyze trades from a biblical perspective to determine their legality by applying five basic rules.

Rule #1: The trade must be conducted according to a legitimate source of binding law. (jurisdictional authority)

Rule #2: The participants in the trade must have the right to offer and receive the item being traded. (legal stewardship)

Rule #3: The participants in the trade must understand and agree to the terms of the trade. (informed consent)

Rule #4: The participants in the trade must not be under duress or subject to any unfair disadvantage in negotiations. (equal bargaining power)

Rule #5: After the trade, the item traded will become an asset for the kingdom that the receiving party is building. (contract fulfillment)

Most people have a general sense of these legal principles. For followers of Jesus, our point of reference for defining the rules of the trade is not man's law but the principles and covenants God established in His word. That brings us to another legal principle that is critical to our discussion. *Stare decisis*. The Cornell Law School defines it as follows.

"Stare decisis is the doctrine that courts will adhere to precedent in making their decisions. Stare decisis means "to stand by things decided" in Latin. When a court faces a legal argument, if a previous court has ruled on the same or a closely related issue, then the court will make their decision in alignment with the previous court's decision."[36]

This important principle directly involves legal rule #1, which identifies the legitimate source of binding law. Now, this may seem obvious, but for followers of Jesus, *the jurisdiction is the Kingdom of God, and thus His Word is the only legitimate foundation for "all things decided*." Any law, principle, or precedent not in alignment with what God established "in the beginning" is illegal and non-binding in His Kingdom. It matters not whether the kings of the earth, or any other authority delegated by them, write laws to the contrary.

When examining economic and trade laws, applying *stare decisis* requires us to return to the original source and determine the original intent of the law-giving body. Our law-giving body is God. The text of the law is the Bible. When applied to economics, that takes us first to John 1:1-5 and Genesis 1 and 2. This is where God established His Covenant (binding

---

[36] https://www.law.cornell.edu/wex/stare_decisis

law) with humanity and revealed the principles that enable us to honor His covenants.

Trading Floors: Where Heaven Meets Earth in Economic Reality

All of this leads to a simple concept I develop across my three books. It is the assertion that every economic exchange includes profound spiritual outcomes. This is because all value exchanges happen on what I call *trading floors.* These are places where any two or more human beings come together and exchange value. The exchange may involve goods, services, money, or non-tangible value that impacts a person's emotional, physical, and spiritual well-being.

In financial terminology, a trading floor is the physical or virtual space where buyers and sellers exchange items with value, such as stocks, bonds, and commodities. I extend this concept to every human interaction and show how each one creates or destroys value simultaneously in the natural and spiritual realms.

To help you better understand how this works within the context of a biblical economic worldview, consider there are three categories of trading floors:

Internal Trading Floors: These are the spaces where your thoughts, beliefs, memories, desires, and decisions are formed and exchanged. It is where the principle of identity is developed and protected, constructed or deconstructed, where fear replaces faith or faith overcomes fear. It is where the decision is made to exchange the truth for a lie,[37] or a lie for the truth.

You witnessed this trading floor in action in the Garden when Eve lost the battle and believed Satan when he told her that she too could "be like the Most High." For today's followers of Jesus, inputs and pressures from secular culture become the enemy's "offer" to make a similar trade. We must constantly manage these trading floors to maintain our identity as a person made in God's image and the worldview that flows from it. The trades made on your internal trading floor determine your identity, and therefore, the kingdom your resources will build. You cannot escape from that reality.

Relational Trading Floors: These are the spaces within families, friendships, and communities where relational value is created and exchanged. James 3 discusses the power of the tongue. We don't normally associate this passage with its impact on building or destroying human identity in an "economic" trade. However, consider that many of our conversations include an act of service or neglect, an expression of forgiveness or bitterness, or contain a word of encouragement or criticism.

Regardless of their impact, large or small, these form what I call "micro-deposits" of blessing or cursing.[38] On relational trading floors, Holy Spirit uses them to build emotional and spiritual well-being, or

---

[37] Romans 1:25

[38] James 3:9,10

Satan uses them to steal, kill, or destroy it. Both directly impact a person's resiliency to identity theft, and therefore, ultimately determine the kingdom which they will build with their resources.

Marketplace Trading Floors: These are the conventional commercial arenas where we exchange currency for goods and services. Because they generally involve transactions made with national currencies, they are the floors that secular economists focus on almost exclusively. They quantify trade conducted with metrics such as Return on Investment (ROI) and Gross Domestic Product (GDP).

While mainly transactional in nature, marketplace trading floors are inseparable from the relational and internal trading floors that precede and surround them. A marketplace built on mere transactions neglects relationships. A scarcity mindset motivates extraction and domination because the person sees the transaction as a zero-sum game where one "wins" and another "loses."

This thinking produces very different outcomes than marketplace exchanges that are built on trust, prioritize care for human identity, and come from an abundance mindset. When these are included, it alters the rules of marketplace trading floors. The sum of the exchange produces value greater than the whole due to simultaneously building human value on relational and personal trading floors.

Satan understands the interrelationships between the three types of trading floors better than we do. He directs the kings of the earth to design economic and monetary systems that give him access to all three. By gaining access to people's thoughts about themselves (internal) and others (relational), he shapes their identity, and thus the values and assumptions that drive their marketplace behavior. By keeping internal and relational trading floors separate from the marketplace trading floor, the economy devolves into a sterile experience focused on advancing materialism and satisfying individual wants. Once again, I refer you to the BBC documentary, "*The Century of the Self.*" If you want to see this in action, please watch the first two videos.

Thankfully, Jesus understands these trading floors better than either us or Satan. In His economic teachings, He constantly included management of internal and relational trading floors. The Sermon on the Mount addresses how we manage our internal trading floors. It addresses worry (identity), anger (relational fragmentation), greed (ownership mindset), and anxiety about provision (scarcity). Jesus knows that if these are all managed properly, value exchanged on marketplace trading floors will naturally align with Kingdom outcomes.

It is past time for followers of Jesus to make the connection between Jesus' teachings and trading floors. Doing so will end the effective theft of resources on trading floors designed by the kings of the earth. A good place to start is by understanding…

Micro-Deposits and the Currency of Love

Micro-deposits of blessing and cursing, which I discussed above, are one of the most practical and powerful tools every follower of Jesus can use to bring about Kingdom economic restoration. When you examine Jesus' life and teachings, you see Him making these "deposits" on nearly every page of the gospels. Jesus was the master at giving an encouraging word, returning a patient response when provocation was expected, performing a generous act when scarcity seemed to prevail, and forgiving when retaliation seemed justified.

When He made these micro-deposits, the results were immediate and consequential. When followers of Jesus begin making consistent micro-deposits of blessing in families, friendships, and communities, it will change the world. Over months and years, they will compound into relational wealth that transforms the character of communities and enables the kind of trust-based cooperation on which God's economy thrives.

The reason is simple. Micro-deposits are 100% relational and they are traded in an abundant spiritual currency known as *love*. Not sentiment or emotion—the love described in 1 Corinthians 13, which is patient, kind, not self-seeking, not easily angered, and keeps no record of wrongs. This kind of love is not a scarce resource. It is not depleted from our "account" when we give it away. In fact, it is available to every follower of Jesus in *infinite supply* through the fruit of the Holy Spirit,[39] who generously pours God's love into our hearts.[40]

Every other form of value that humans create and exchange is limited. Time, money, energy, attention—all are finite. But love is a fruit of the Spirit and is therefore genuinely inexhaustible. A person who has access to an unlimited currency and understands how to deploy it wisely, on the proper trading floors, and at the right time, holds a form of economic power that no system devised by man can replicate or suppress.

When followers of Jesus begin to practice this at scale, it will dismantle Satan's ability to steal human identity and instead empower humans to unleash the image of God into the world and become members of God's Kingdom. People in communities will develop genuine trust. Cooperation will then become embedded in their spiritual DNA, displacing the spirits of competition and control. Generosity will flow where scarcity thinking previously constrained. Over time, trade will flow freely between local communities, creating a resilient "economic ecosystem" that will withstand the shaking of man's failing systems and yet another "Great Reset."

It is my firm belief that a large-scale understanding and embrace of a biblical economic worldview that unleashes these micro-deposits will be a game changer for the Kingdom of God. And there is absolutely nothing the enemy can do to stop it.

---

[39] Galatians 5:22,23
[40] Romans 5:5

Breaking Spiritual Inertia: The Challenge of Transformation at Scale

I fully believe that it is possible to accomplish what I just stated. However, intellectually understanding the principles of kingdom building, trading floors, and micro-deposits is not the same as applying them. Between intellectual understanding and consistent practice lies one of the most formidable laws of nature: inertia.

To give you an idea of how I approach the subject, I will quote the opening paragraph of Chapter 25, in *I Came to Give*, which is entitled "Build a New Ecosystem."

"For thousands of years, human beings have lived with economic systems based on control and competition. The enemy has created an enormous quantity of spiritual and cultural inertia during this time. Overcoming it will require time and patience as we develop, test, correct, and deploy the tools needed to render to God a new system based on cooperation, stewardship, abundance, identity, and sustainability."

In the physical realm, inertia is the tendency of objects to maintain their current state of motion unless acted upon by an external force. Spiritual and cultural inertia is the tendency of individuals, families, churches, and communities to maintain their current patterns of thinking and behavior, even when it is clearly misaligned with God's design and intent.

When applied to economics, spiritual and cultural inertia is not simply a moral failure. It is the accumulated energy of generations of grossly distorted economic worldviews, reinforced by economic systems that consistently reward conformity to Satan's principles. The person who hoards in a scarcity economy often does better in the short term than the person who gives generously. The business that competes ruthlessly is often more "profitable" than the one that cooperates sacrificially. The individual who claims ownership aggressively accumulates more "stuff" than the one who sows their resources generously into the Kingdom. The consequences of these short-term incentives and misaligned definitions of prosperity compound across generations until the system that created them feels, not just normal, but desirable.

Changing this directional momentum will require enormous counter-spiritual energy. Thankfully, there is no greater source of power than the Word of God. A clear vision, a compelling narrative, practical tools, strong community support, and the persistent application of God's principles over time will ultimately prevail.

This kind of change demands a Spirit-driven, community-oriented, and narrative-sustained shift in how followers of Jesus think and act economically. The shift begins when believers discover a hidden truth: there are foundational problems with the way we create, steward, and exchange value in our daily lives, and these problems have a direct and profound impact on the Kingdom we claim to serve.

Yet discovering this truth is not enough. It must lead to decisive action. We must commit to live differently, demonstrating through visible results that God's economic principles actually work. When we do, our churches and communities will become magnetic centers of hope for those disillusioned with today's secular economic systems. That is when economic transformation begins to scale.

Chapter 4
God's Principles and History

"Thus says the LORD, 'Stand by the ways and see and ask for the ancient paths, Where the good way is, and walk in it;
And you will find rest for your souls.'"
Jeremiah 6:16a

The majority of *I Came to Give* is the account of how God's economic principles came into being and the result of what happened when they were, or were not, applied throughout history. It is impossible to cover it in detail here. However, because of the challenges we face today, it is important that you know at least some of this history.

In chapter two of this book, I explained how Satan gained a foothold in the world's economic system. In this chapter I will provide an overview of how Satan's principalities and powers became masters over today's economic and monetary systems over the last three thousand years.

Before beginning, I need to summarize important context that is fully developed in my other three books, starting with a review of the first three of the ten commandments.

"Then God spoke all these words, saying, 'I am the LORD your God, who brought you out of the land of Egypt, out of the house of slavery. 'You shall have no other gods before Me. 'You shall not make for yourself an idol, or any likeness of what is in heaven above or on the earth beneath or in the water under the earth. You shall not worship them or serve them; for I, the LORD your God, am a jealous God, visiting the iniquity of the fathers on the children, on the third and the fourth generations of those who hate Me, but showing lovingkindness to thousands, to those who love Me and keep My commandments. 'You shall not take the name of the LORD your God in vain, for the LORD will not leave him unpunished who takes His name in vain."
Exodus 20:1-7

Keep these commandments in mind as we jump to the book of Deuteronomy, where a major meta-theme becomes clear, beginning in chapter four. God gives Israel a specific and urgent exhortation (paraphrasing of course): Remember My statutes! Do not add to them or take away from them! Do not forget all that you have seen and all that I have done for you! Remember the Ten Commandments![41]

The remainder of chapter four focuses almost exclusively on upholding the first three commandments. You are entering into a land where the people have worshiped false gods, idols, and images of all kinds for generations. I plead with you, do not

[41] Deuteronomy 4:1-14

worship them! This chapter sets a pattern that continues through the following *eight* chapters. God continually urges them to follow His statutes and warns about idol worship.

Please note: Over thirty percent of Deuteronomy focuses on driving home the importance of keeping the first three commandments. Generational blessings of obedience and generational curses of disobedience are the consequences of success or failure. God makes clear His disdain for false images because of whom they represent and what they do to His people.

> "The graven images of their gods you are to burn with fire; you shall not covet the silver or the gold that is on them, nor take it for yourselves, or you will be snared by it, for it is an abomination to the LORD your God. You shall not bring an abomination into your house, and like it come under the ban; you shall utterly detest it, and you shall utterly abhor it, for it is something banned."
> Deuteronomy 7:25-26

What does all of this have to do with economics? A lot, as it turns out. Keep these passages in mind as you read through the historical account that I present here. Also, know that as you read, there are assertions and conclusions made that are supported by dozens of footnotes linked to Scripture and other sources that I have documented in *I Came to Give*. What follows is a summarized historical account, in chronological order. It begins at approximately 700 B.C.

- Isaiah 46 opens by drawing Israel's attention specifically to idols that bear the images of beasts and cattle.[42] God then personally speaks a prophecy about money, using a now-familiar phrase to ensure their attention is where it needs to be.

"To whom will you liken Me, and make Me equal And compare Me, that we should be alike? They lavish gold out of the bag, And weigh silver on the scales; They hire a goldsmith, and he makes it a god; They prostrate themselves, yes, they worship."
Isaiah 46:5-6 (NKJV)

Note: The Hebrew word for "liken" used in verse 5 is the same Hebrew word used in Isaiah 14 when Satan declared he would "be like" the Most High. It means "to pursue with passion becoming the image of something else" to usurp their position, purpose, and person.

- Archaeologists and historians agree that the images first stamped on coins minted in Lydia were of animals, just as Isaiah had prophesied:

"Bel has bowed down, Nebo stoops over; Their images are consigned to the beasts and the cattle..."
Isaiah 46:1

[42] Isaiah 46:1

(Sixth Century B.C. Lydian Coins)

- Imaged coins became a symbol of power in city-states and regions. Over time, minters were directed to stamp images of pagan gods and government rulers on them rather than animals. Soon, nearly all coins bore images of secular rulers.

(Fourth Century B.C. Coin minted in Corinth)

- Money changers understood the differences in the value of various coins stamped with the images of self-proclaimed gods. Both the coins and the money changers became critical components in Satan's emerging monetary system. The use of god-imaged coins for trade steadily expanded. Just as Satan planned, the geographic territory impacted by their use expanded also.

- There is a little known, yet critical period, in economic and monetary history that began in 166 B.C. During the Hasmonean dynasty, a small group of Jewish priests had seen enough of the spiritual damage these coins created. They rejected coins bearing the images of gods and men and created their own coins with images that conformed to Jewish Law.

Most of their new coins bore the image of a double cornucopia with a pomegranate nestled in the middle. Note that these images symbolized abundance to the Jewish people.

- Jesus grew up in territory controlled by the Roman Empire. His family put food on the table by participating in an economic system designed to advance Caesar's kingdom. The coins He and His family traded for food, clothing, and shelter bore an image and an inscription that declared Caesar was a "god." Every day, Jesus watched His friends and family struggle under oppression due to the generational curse of a monetary system that was an abomination to God and an affront to His Son.

- Jesus, King of the world, twice overturned the money changers tables in the temple. Understanding the history of image stamped coins helps us understand why. The official coin accepted for payment of the temple tax was the half-shekel pictured below. It was minted in Tyre. On the front was the god Melqart, proclaimed to be "king of the city of Tyre." Recall who else the king of Tyre represented? Satan was thrusting his power over the economic and monetary systems directly into the face of God's people.

- When confronted by the Pharisees about taxes, Jesus asked them to bring Him a denarius so that He could "see" it.[43] Below is a picture of that coin.

The Greek word for "see" it is *horáō* and it means "properly see, to see with the mind, perceive with inward spiritual perception." Jesus then asked them a question. "Whose image and inscription is this?" They replied "Caesar's."

Consider what follows in the context of what Scripture and history have revealed thus far about coinage. The inscription read, "Tiberivs Caesar Divi Avgvsti Filivs Avgvstvs" or "Caesar Augustus Tiberius, son of the Divine Augustus." There stood Jesus, the Son of the one true God, holding a Roman coin which bore a graven image and an inscription declaring Caesar was the son of a god.

When Jesus answered, "Render to Caesar the things that are Caesar's, and to God the things that are God's," it was not about something as trivial as "love God and pay your taxes." The Pharisees would

[43] Mark 12:13-17 NKJV

have immediately connected the coin's image and inscription to the first three commandments, which forbids graven images and worship of idols and false gods. They would have understood the implications of such an image on the coin used for the temple tax. And, they would have recalled what the Jewish high priests did during the Hasmonean Dynasty when faced with this same reality. Now, *that* would have "amazed them."[44]

- The spread of god-imaged, generationally cursed coins continued to proliferate throughout the known world. Governments found clever ways to "debase" the coins by diluting the content of the silver or gold from which they were made. Under the reign of Marcus Aurelius (161-180 A.D), the content of silver in the denarius dropped from over 95% to 75%.[45] The reason they debased the coins was to create more "money" to fund war and expand the Roman Empire.
- Satan was not just active in biblical geographic territory. Around the year 800 A.D. his demonic spirits convinced the Chinese people that they preferred "paper" sacrifices rather than traditional high-value tangible items. It is documented that the spirits said: "I have no use for your copper cash; I desire cash only made from white paper."[46] This is how paper money was introduced into the world.

---

[44] Mark 12:17

[45] Bruce Bartlett, *How Excessive Government Killed Ancient Rome*, 294

[46] *A Study and Translation of Tang Lin's Ming-pao Chi*, 254

- For the next eight hundred years, paper money caused incredible hardship for the Chinese people. Printing new notes was easier than debasing coins made of precious metals. Multiple accounts of complete financial collapse are recorded. Finally, the hardship caused by its use became too much and in 1636, paper money was outlawed in China.
- Marco Polo learned about paper money during his travels to China and introduced it to the West. Leaders there rejected it initially, saying "The doge (chief magistrate of Venise) and the cardinal (Pope's cousin) looked at these notes in awe and dismay. The hen scratch writing was not in Latin or Greek but in a secret language, most likely the language of the devil." They proceeded to burn the notes and accused Polo of heresy. [47] At least someone in history had eyes to "*horáō*" it!
- In 1690, government officials in the colony of Massachusetts printed the first fiat paper money in the Western world. They used it to pay their soldiers to go to war.
- In 1775 paper money was created by the colonies to fund the Revolutionary War.
- In 1862 President Lincoln's Legal Tender Act allowed the National Treasury to issue paper money to fund the Civil War.

---

[47] The Book of Ser Marco Polo, 423-426

(Yes, paper money had its own images and inscriptions, perpetuating the generational curse. Do you see the trend here? Government-debased image-cursed coins and paper money were consistently issued to conduct war and kill humans.)

- Today, the masters of our monetary system create money and currency, not by pouring metal or even printing paper, but by making a computer entry on a keyboard. That keyboard entry creates a new loan to an individual, business, or government. Each unit of money you have stored in your bank account is nothing more than a claim on a debt owed by someone else.

  The implications of this are difficult for most people to grasp. In reality, today's monetary system makes nearly everyone in the world a debt slave. Trillions of various currencies are created every year by keystroke entries to buy government debt to fund programs that run counter to dearly held Christian values: abortion, DEI, usurpation of jurisdictional authority, and of course, unending war.

If you recall from the Introduction, I said we have been given an opportunity that comes along once every few generations to make changes to our economic and monetary systems. The reason was because of their consistent abuse, overreach, and subsequent failure. This brief historical account provides some of the "receipts" documented in *I Came to Give* to support that claim.

Today's system is on the verge of another reset. The World Economic Forum and United Nations talk about it openly. While this knowledge can cause one to fall into fear, the historical record also shows that local communities are not powerless when man's systems fail. We will look at two examples that are instructive for us as this next "reset" unfolds.

The Central Middle Ages

One of the most striking historical examples I draw upon is the remarkable economic and cultural flourishing of medieval Europe between roughly 1050-1300 AD. The collapse of the Roman Empire and the fallout from the Black Death decimated humanity for centuries. However, historians discovered that people living in Europe experienced a degree of abundance and prosperity in stark contrast to that of the rest of the region. [48]

Between 1180 and 1230, many universities were founded in Europe.[49] There was a large increase in private ownership of land, and in many cases, crop yields more than doubled.[50]

According to medievalist R. Phillippe, in France, there were 20,000 water mills built. Local communities successfully funded specific projects to

---

[48] Bernard Lietaer, New Money for a New World, Kindle location 1170-1280

[49] Guy Bois, La Grande Dépression Médiévale – le XIV–XVeme siècle: le Précédent d'une crise systémique (Paris: PUF, 2000), 11

[50] Bois, La Grande Depression, 15

benefit their citizens.[51] By the year 1300, almost one thousand cathedrals had been built in Western Europe, along with a house of worship for every two hundred people. [52]

Where did this enormous investment of resources and creative energy come from? Not by central planning or from a government subsidy. It was instead funded by a sophisticated network of local, community-issued, complementary currencies that circulated within various regions. These currencies were not backed by gold or issued by kings. They were backed by the productive capacity of local communities and managed by local guilds and churches.

The results were extraordinary. Historical accounts describe an era of high employment, abundant food, high wages for skilled workers, remarkable innovations in art and architecture, and vibrant community life. The cathedral builders were not serfs working under compulsion. Many were skilled craftsmen who earned good wages and belonged to guilds that provided training, mutual aid, and community cohesiveness. Construction of these massive buildings was, in many communities, an organized economic project that spanned multiple generations—a form of long-term, cooperative investment in something greater than any individual or family.

---

[51] R. Philippe, *L'Énergie au Moyen Age: L'Exemple des Pays d'Entre Seine et Loire de la fin du XIeme Siècle a la fin du XVeme Siècle* (Paris: 1982).

[52] Georges Duby, *L'Europe des Cathedrales*: (1966) 1140-1290

Unfortunately, their prosperity did not last. During the thirteenth century, the doctrine of "king by divine right" was imposed. Central authorities overruled the decisions of local governments. King Louis IX of France decreed that only royal mints had the right to issue coins throughout the realm, thus abolishing the use of local currencies. The results were predictable.

Abolishing local currencies caused subsequent generations to suffer from famine, unsanitary conditions, epidemics, and death. Between 1315 and 1317, a Great Famine in Europe claimed nearly ten percent of the population.[53] Then, in 1347, the Black Death gained a foothold in Crimea. From there, it quickly spread throughout Europe.

Several historians have taken a second look at the period between 1200 to 1400 and concluded that if the economy had remained strong and the people healthy, the death toll from the Plague could have been significantly reduced. Decades of economic decline had dramatically weakened the physical and emotional well-being of the population, and their bodies and minds could not mount a defense.

I do not claim that medieval Europe's economy was fully based on biblical principles. It was deeply flawed in many ways—hierarchical, often exploitative, centralized, and violent. But embedded within its economic system were functional prototypes of God's cooperative and stewardship principles, made possible by locally managed, community-serving

---

[53] Henry S. Lucas, "The Great European Famine of 1315-1316", Speculum 5, no. 4, 343-77

monetary instruments. When they were replaced by centralized, scarcity-based money, the cooperative economy they sustained collapsed—exactly as God's principles predict.

The German Wara (1929-1931)

Prior to the Great Depression, the largest employer in the community of Schwanenkirchen was the local coal mine. As post-World War I German hyperinflation began, the mine was forced to file for bankruptcy and halt operations.

A resident of Schwanenkirchen proposed backing a local community currency system with coal from the local mine. Coal held value that the community understood. Backing the paper scrip with coal would provide a measure of credibility. He told the community's citizens that the currency system would only work if they and other businesses would accept payment in the scrip, which he called the "Wara." The residents decided they had nothing to lose, so they said yes. That choice changed their lives.

The Wara scrip was a huge success. It saved the coal mine and revitalized the local economy. It was so successful that surrounding communities began using it. Soon, it circulated throughout the nation. Banks even opened accounts that accepted the Wara. And that turned out to be its downfall.

The German Central Bank became concerned about its popularity and declared the Wara, and other local currencies, illegal. Once again, the kings of the earth removed a threat to their monetary monopoly, plunging their citizens back into poverty. The central government's abuse of power created widespread disillusionment and anger. A dramatic shift began to take hold in the German political landscape. In its wake, the Nazi party and Hitler rose to power.

Can we blame the rise of Hitler solely on the decision by the German government to ban local currencies? No. Did it play a role? Absolutely. Did banning the Wara create unnecessary human suffering and misery? Again, absolutely. Are these facts printed in our history books? No, they are not. Why?

God's purpose for money is very different than man's. I include these examples to demonstrate that the kings of the earth design their monetary systems to assert centralized control and make monetary items scarce. This enables the enemy to enter the picture and drive people to succumb to the spirits of control and competition in their pursuit of these resources.

Meanwhile, when God's principles are applied to money it creates a very different outcome. Consider that the Hebrew word for "coin" is *zuz,* and it means to "move" or "circulate." God wants *all* currencies, national, local, and micro, to freely flow throughout our communities. This facilitates cooperation and stewardship as we create abundant, stable, resilient assets for His Kingdom. Not through control and scarcity, but through radically empowering love.

Chapter 5

The Covenant, Creation, and the Opportunity Ahead

"The Lord said, 'Behold, they are one people, and they all have the same language. And this is what they began to do, and now nothing which they purpose to do will be impossible for them.'"
Genesis 11:6

In chapter one, I introduced "The Covenant." You may have connected some of the consequences of breaking the Covenant to the events covered over the last few chapters. However, we have only scratched the surface. To illustrate this, we will return to the biblical historical narrative in Genesis 6.

Within two thousand years of the creation of man, humanity and the earth had been corrupted to the point that there was no practical path to restoration. Humanity had completely ignored the Covenant to serve and protect Creation and to steward the abundant resources provided to build God's Kingdom. God's response was revealing.

Genesis 6:6 says He was *grieved* in His heart and *sorry* that He had made man. The Hebrew word for "grieved" is *âṣaḇ*, and it indicates deep emotional pain. The Hebrew word for "sorry" is *nâḥam*, and it means to sigh as moved with compassion to repentance.

The intensity of God's lament reveals His deep love for His Son, humanity, and Creation and the sadness He felt over the breakdown in the relationships the Covenant was meant to hold together. Sin was so widespread that He could no longer watch Creation and humanity continue to suffer the consequences. Something had to change. Therefore, God declared that He would establish a new covenant with humanity[54] and Creation, whereby He would ensure the circumstances that led to the need to destroy the world He loves, and its inhabitants,[55] would never be repeated.

It is incredible that God had the foresight to design Creation in such a way that it could still produce in abundance after such a catastrophic event as a global flood. It allowed Him to restate the original mandate given in Genesis 1:28—with some conditions. He reminded Noah that Creation is His gift to humanity and that it will provide them with abundant food. He also informed Noah of specific and strict consequences of defiling the land through the shedding of innocent blood. Then God unilaterally established His new Covenant with both humanity and Creation.[56]

---

[54] Genesis 6:18
[55] John 3:16
[56] Genesis 9:1-7

This was indeed a new beginning. However, for Creation to produce the resources necessary to fulfill the restated mission of Genesis 1:28, humanity needed to repent. Serving and protecting the earth needed to be reestablished *as a centering point* for relationships between humans, God, Jesus, and Creation. Embracing God's economic principles of cooperation, stewardship, abundance, protection from identity theft, and sustainability is how humanity would honor the new Covenant for generations.

Unfortunately, you do not have to read much further in Genesis to see that humanity failed again to uphold the new Covenant. Economic systems soon became dominated again by the enemy's principles of control, competition, ownership, scarcity, identity theft, and fragility. To this day, humanity has struggled to build an economic system that incorporates even some of God's principles.

Where We Are Today

The church has failed to grasp the enormous cost to humanity and Creation that has resulted from repeatedly failing to honor the Covenant. We now live in a world where war, abortion, and cultural genocide committed against indigenous people have spilled so much innocent blood that cries from the earth once again continually fill God's ears.[57] Adding to the "curse," aggressive tilling practices and mono-crop farming have been adopted worldwide over the last

[57] Genesis 4:9-10, Genesis 5

century.[58] What was once deep, lively, nutrient-rich topsoil is now shallow and nearly dead.

Today, much of the world's farmland acts only as a temporary holder for root systems of genetically modified plants. Each plant requires a toxic brew of chemicals and artificial fertilizers to produce its yield. The result is that the land is being forced to "give up its strength" against its will and natural use. The same can be said for animals raised in confined, assembly line production stalls. Their lives are disrespected and the natural expression of how God created them is hidden from view. In each case, this constitutes physical abuse every bit as real and wrongful as when it is inflicted on human beings.

Our utter failure to serve and protect Creation has decimated it on a scale we cannot comprehend. To say it groans for redemption[59] is an understatement. The cost to the human side of the ledger is just as staggering. Large corporate food production, processing, and distribution systems have disconnected most humans from the intimate relationship God intended them to have with Creation, and through it, with His Son. They produce highly processed foods that are laced with additives and preservatives and provide little nutritional value. These systems now dominate our centralized and fragile food supply chain. They are directly responsible for a growing health crisis in nations

---

[58] https://www.sciencenews.org/article/soil-erosion-rate-us-midwest-unsustainable-usda

[59] Romans 8:19-22

worldwide, while they simultaneously generate enormous profits for both “Big Ag” and “Big Pharma.”

Adding to humanity’s woes is the fact that most people rarely, if ever, touch the soil with the intention to cultivate and keep it. Instead, they have turned their attention to consuming “stuff” created by an economic system that has become efficient at extracting natural, non-reproducible elements from the land and converting them into products that provide little real utility value. The system then disposes of the waste, without considering its impact on Creation and future generations.

This is just a small sliver of the brutal *economic* reality we live with today. The *cultural* reality is just as brutal. Take for example the precipitous decline of family cohesion. A study published in the *Journal of Adolescent Health* found that frequent family meals are associated with lower rates of depression and suicidal thoughts among adolescents.[60] Yet today, many busy and distracted parents no longer know the joy of preparing meals for their families. Instead, they consider it a burden to do so.

This is the direct result of losing our connection with the Covenant and the relationships God intended it to nurture. Instead, we have become slaves to an economic system that is intentionally designed to steal, kill, and destroy natural and human resources by any means possible. It is tragic that not only do most

---

[60] Eisenberg, M. E., Olson, R. E., Neumark-Sztainer, D., Story, M., & Bearinger, L. H. (2004). Correlations Between Family Meals and Psychosocial Well-being Among Adolescents.

followers of Jesus fail to understand this, but they embrace the enemy's system because of the "stuff" it produces to satisfy their flesh.

Therefore, absent an immediate course correction, the world will continue to move into an extended period of cultural, geopolitical, and economic decline—and transition. A friend and mentor of mine, Dennis Peacocke, foresaw this in 2012. In his book, *On the Destiny of Nations – Resolving Our Economic Crisis* Dennis outlined the three phases through which we would pass as the transition unfolds.

Phase One: Economic Stagnation, Denial, and Insufficient Remedies - In managing the global economy, central governments and the central banks of the world have ignored the five principles of kingdom building and broken the Covenant. Rather than acknowledge their error, they deny their role in the unfolding global chaos as they plan to take unprecedented control over the global economy—and much more—via their "Great Reset."

In this phase, as instability grows, citizens will clamor for stability and safety. Many nations will see leaders thrown out in favor of those who tell their citizens that their plan will make their pain go away. Their proposals will promise outcomes that, for many, will sound attractive. However, they will only serve to expand their power and control. Within that framework, phase two will begin.

Phase Two: The Bridge Period Between the Old and New Normal - Government officials at all levels worldwide will begin to publicly acknowledge the issues that citizens are already aware of. Supply chains, including those related to food, will begin to break down due to global and domestic conflict. Unemployment will rise along with food prices.

As economic stagnation intensifies, some governments will propose "universal basic income" to aid families suffering from unemployment and inflation. Fragile cooperation between nations will falter as a scarcity mindset drives national leaders into self-preservation mode. Long-standing national alliances will break down and new ones will form, further adding to geopolitical and economic instability.

Citizens will become disillusioned with central governments and central banks. Because of the policy failures of these institutions, citizens will transfer governing authority to leaders within their states, providences, counties, and communities in areas previously controlled exclusively by centralized powers. This will include management of their local economies. During this phase people will be most open to "radical" ideas to solve the deep structural problems within the existing economic and monetary systems.

Phase Three: The New Normal - In his book, Dennis provides a concise description of what we can expect in the final phase:

> "[During this phase we] will begin the journey of living out the consequent changes [society] has had to make to reorder its economic and political philosophies concerning the roles of its citizens and the functional abilities of civil government to support them. Local communities will not soon give up their newfound powers after having fought their battles to achieve power and survive."[61]

Leaders in many local communities will take responsibility for their citizens' well-being on a scale not witnessed in at least a century. Their ability to maintain their hard-won jurisdictional authority will be, in large part, determined by two factors.

- The trust built between the citizens and their local leaders during phase two.
- The principles upon which their economic and social frameworks are built.

The success, or failure, of maintaining local jurisdictional authority will have profound consequences that will last for generations. As of 2026, the world is transitioning from Phase One to Phase Two. This provides followers of Jesus with a historic opportunity over the coming months and years to present God's radical ways as the path forward and establish the ekklesia as a source of wisdom.

Before that can happen, followers of Jesus must first practice what they will preach. This means

[61] Dennis Peacocke, *On the Destiny of Nations*, (2012), 49

establishing a parallel economy grounded in God's principles that will demonstrate a viable alternative to dependence on the debt-based, scarcity-enforcing, fragility-prone economic system of Satan's kingdom.

A Thief in the Movement

One of the most theologically interesting observations I make in *Cultivate and Keep* is the recognition that God's principles can be—and often are—discovered and applied by people who are not aware of their divine origin. There is a worldwide proliferation of initiatives combining environmental stewardship with local economic development: community-supported agriculture, local food networks, regenerative farming practices, community investment funds, local currency experiments, cooperative businesses, and similar efforts.

This sounds great at first. Unfortunately, most of these initiatives are led by people with a predominantly secular worldview. Many are motivated by concerns about climate change, equity, inclusion, and social justice—not by building a Kingdom for our King. Yet in their models, they often include God's principles of cooperation and a belief in abundance, while focusing on serving their local communities.

Many followers of Jesus are content to apply Paul's words from Philippians 1:18 to these initiatives: "What then? Only that in every way, whether in pretense or in truth, Christ [God's economic principles] is proclaimed; and in this I rejoice."

I am sorry, but this attitude is rubbish. Can we learn from these people? Yes, of course. However, when secular organizations "preach" stewardship of nature through regenerative agricultural practices, they often worship the creature rather than the Creator. As a result, their message does not lead people to Christ. This is yet another reason why the body of Christ needs to see the world through the lens of a biblical economic worldview. Only by doing so can we create a new framework for restoration that is not obscured and confused by the secular traditions of men but instead gives glory and honor to our King and Creator.

Chapter 6
The Restoration Framework

"that He may send Jesus, the Christ appointed for you, whom heaven must receive until the period of restoration of all things about which God spoke by the mouth of His holy prophets from ancient time."
Acts 3:20-21

While man clamors about his economic "Great Reset," I believe God is asking us to join Him in something very different — a "Great Restoration" of His economic principles and ways. This will require commitment, preparation, planning, and persistence. At Regeneco you will find pathways that equip leaders of households, churches, communities, and nations as they engage in this restoration process. These pathways are not rigid formulas, but adaptable frameworks that can be shaped and molded to fit each person's unique circumstances as they serve in their God-given spheres of jurisdiction.

This brings up a subject I did not develop in my first three books. That is the theology behind biblical jurisdiction. In the Bible, the words jurisdiction and authority are often interchanged. Simply put, a jurisdiction is a geographic or relational sphere of influence and authority that has been delegated to an individual or council. The key word is "delegated."

While beyond the scope of this book, Scripture provides guidance on how and by whom this authority is delegated, and there are many good resources that will help you to better understand it. For our purposes, it is important to understand how we serve people within specific spheres of jurisdiction to achieve the restoration of God's economic principles and ways. As such, let's identify the most common jurisdictions in which we operate.

- The first sphere is the individual, a single autonomous human being.
- The second is the household, which generally, but not exclusively, consists of family members.
- The third is the local church. This does not mean a single congregation, but rather the ekklesia, which means a "governing body" in a community that will include people from many congregations.
- The fourth is the local community. Generally, it is defined by geography and may include several local townships and villages, especially in rural areas.
- The final jurisdiction is a nation. We think of these as defined by geography as well. However, in some circumstances they may be better defined as a strongly delineated ethic group that shares a common culture and language.

Advancing on Multiple Fronts

Economic transformation in each jurisdiction will include a diverse set of participants. There will be a variety of doctrinal beliefs, levels of maturity and commitment, and priorities. Those leading the transformation process must understand this and be prepared to meet and serve people where they are.

The goal is to serve each person as they travel their respective pathway. As they do, relational and economic networks will begin to form. Regeneco will help facilitate the convergence of participants at specific points along the way. Ultimately, the objective is to create a local economic ecosystem that will transform families, churches, communities, nations, and the Kingdom of God for generations. Following is a framework for pathways in each jurisdiction:

Individual/Household Leaders

1. Learn: Worldview awareness
    - Books and Foundations video series
    - Personal application of basic principles
2. Assess: Commitment, capabilities, capacity
    - Resources available
3. Share: Recruit others to begin their own journey
4. Connect: Join/form trade network

Local Church Leaders

1. Learn: Worldview awareness
    - Books and Foundations video series
    - Personal application of basic principles

2. Assess: Commitment, capabilities, capacity
    - Determine practical pathway to adoption
    - Inventory the assets of the church and congregation
3. Empower: Internal validation
    - Unleash the Champion to advance the project within the church.
    - Support group studies or form a committee
4. Connect: Join/form/expand a growing trade network

Local Community/County Leaders

1. Learn: Worldview awareness
    - Books and Foundations video series
    - Personal application of basic principles
2. Assess: Commitment, capabilities, capacity
3. Convene: Key people in the community meet, unite and begin to…
4. Collaborate: Lay the foundation for success
    - Form a Local Economic Restoration Team
        - Strategize rollout
        - Assess community capacity and pace
        - Form Prayer Teams
        - Recruit others
        - Educate and cast vision so others can begin their own pathway
5. Converge:
    - Connect all local community participants
    - Coordinate activities and networks
    - Meet with regional/national leaders

State/Providence/National Leaders

1. Learn: Worldview awareness
    - Books and Foundations video series
    - Personal application of basic principles
2. Assess: Commitment, capabilities, capacity
3. Convene: Key leaders meet, unite, and begin to…
4. Collaborate: Lay the foundation for success
    - Form an Economic Restoration Team
        - Strategize coordination
        - Assess capacity and pace
        - Recruit others into the movement
        - Educate and cast vision so they can begin their own pathway
    - Form Prayer Teams
        - Assign strategic targets
5. Converge:
    - Connect local community leaders
    - Coordinate activities and networks
    - Meet with key local leaders

Note the similarities in the pathways, particularly in the early stages. Regardless of the jurisdiction in which you serve, it begins with understanding and adopting the five principles in your personal life. From there, it extends into adopting the principles in organizations (for and non-profit) that you may lead or influence. Regeneco has comprehensive assessments that help you do so with minimal effort and maximum impact. Both personal and organizational adoption are critical to successful long-term local and national economic transformation.

Finally, note the formation of Prayer and Economic Restoration Teams. These are necessary to help coordinate activities and advance the movement by providing structure and continuity. Let's take some time to look at the functions they perform.

The Prayer Team

Every jurisdiction must include people who are trained in how to conduct targeted prayer intercession. Within Prayer Teams, seasoned prayer leaders will appropriately seek God's strategy to identify and engage the principalities and powers that inhabit their jurisdiction. They may include teams who will provide personal prayer cover for church and community leadership and their families. Highly functioning prayer teams will also help leaders in Economic Restoration Teams to discern strategy and timing of key decisions like implementation and recruitment.

Like biblical jurisdiction, the subject of prayer intercession is well beyond the scope of this book. Thankfully, the Lord has brought me into relationships with people and organizations that specialize in preparing community and national teams to wisely enter the spiritual war that will be fought in each jurisdiction.

The Economic Restoration Team

This group is generally made up of leaders from local churches, the civil government, and businesses. It is where relationships and heavenly strategy come together to execute on God's priorities and plans. The members work with Prayer Teams to develop key relationships, teach citizens, formulate strategies and craft practical implementation steps. Their most important function is forming coalitions to implement "boots on the ground" economic transformation initiatives in local communities. This team will include seasoned leaders who know their community's history and have earned the trust and respect of the citizens. There are four critical skillsets that, when all present, will dramatically increase the likelihood of success.

1. The Champion. These people deeply own the vision and enthusiastically communicate it to others.
2. The Convener. These are people who can call meetings, and key people will take heed and attend.
3. The Advancer. These are practitioners who are skilled in project management and will see that plans and strategies are implemented.
4. The Watchman. These people keep abreast of the changing economic and geopolitical conditions that will affect project implementation.

Leaders in both Prayer and Economic Restoration Teams will practice service-based power, based on a love for the people with whom they live. They will naturally prioritize care for the community's real and spiritual orphans and will desire to create a pathway for them to live with dignity.

A restoration framework, consisting of properly formed teams operating within their proper jurisdictions, is vital for successful, sustainable economic transformation, whether in the home, church, community, or nation. Regeneco offers this framework as a starting point and stands ready to help you begin.

Chapter 7
The Hour and the Call

"How blessed is the man who does not walk in the counsel of the wicked, Nor stand in the path of sinners, Nor sit in the seat of scoffers! But his delight is in the law of the LORD, And in His law he meditates day and night. He will be like a tree firmly planted by streams of water, Which yields its fruit in its season And its leaf does not wither; And in whatever he does, he prospers."
Psalms 1:1-3.

You and I are living in a moment of extraordinary challenge and opportunity. The economic systems built on Satan's counterfeit principles are showing their fragility with increasing clarity. The global monetary system's debt-based slavery is oppressing families and communities with relentless pressure. Local economies are hollowing out, as resources flow to distant lands. Creation itself sends unmistakable warning signals that the Covenant has been violated on a massive scale and that changes must happen soon.

Meanwhile, most of the organized church watches from the sidelines. Spiritually unaware and economically illiterate, they preach the abundant life while embracing the very system that produces scarcity and is at war with the Kingdom that they claim to inhabit. However, be encouraged.

God is opening the eyes of His followers around the world to man's "Great Reset" — a plan openly promoted by the World Economic Forum to consolidate greater control over the global economy. In contrast, He is offering His people a powerful alternative: a Great Restoration based on His economic principles and ways.

As the reality of the gospel of the Kingdom takes root in their hearts, believers are discovering the profound, practical implications this has for how they create, steward, and deploy resources. In response, followers of Jesus are beginning to awaken to the reality of our present challenges. Many are joining their secular counterparts by forming local economic alliances and building resilient food supply networks. In the process, they are reconnecting with Creation in ways that visibly demonstrate the power of God's Covenant, His principles, and His radical ways.

As we continue to move through the three economic transitional phases outlined in Chapter 5, the contrast between the Great Reset and the Great Restoration will become increasingly clear to followers of Jesus. Therefore, we must prepare for the long battle to win the hearts and minds of our fellow image bearers by engaging in a persistent pattern of principled persuasion that God's economic design is better than man's. Over the next decade, the degree of success we experience on that front will determine the economic course of history for generations. As we engage in the battle, we can expect to see several developments as indicators of our progress.

Establishing local food systems will emerge as a priority in local communities.

The complexity and fragility of the global food supply chain will become evident in the near term. While it is a major concern, we can focus on the motivation to re-establish local food systems in a way that transcends fear of hardship or scarcity. That is because God has always intended for the production, distribution, and consumption of food to be a cooperative effort that brings together humanity in fellowship with one another as it serves as the foundation of His economic design.

Local food systems connect communities to Creation in direct and tangible ways, build local economic resiliency, create opportunities for cooperative enterprises, and provide visible, accessible demonstrations of love to our neighbors. This is true in good times, bad times, and end times.

We see the importance of food throughout Scripture. The Covenant established in the Creation narrative was the opening act in the story of the role it plays in the biblical narrative. Take for example, the account of Joseph's life documented later in the book of Genesis. His story encompassed nearly one-third of the book and provides a fascinating record of how God used one man to preserve the five economic principles of kingdom building during a critical period in history.

It culminated in his preserving the fledgling nation of Israel through a seven-year famine.

Continuing in the book of Exodus, we see another well-known account that takes on new meaning when examined through the lens of a biblical economic worldview. I am sure you are familiar with the miracles of the ten plagues, which resulted in Pharoah's release of the Israelites after four hundred and thirty years in bondage. This release is still remembered to this day during the celebration of Passover. For many, that is the point, and thus the end of the story. However, let's take a moment to consider the practical reality of what those plagues meant to the lives of all who lived in Egypt.

- Blood filled the water, which killed the fish and made it unsuitable for drinking and irrigating their crops.
- Frogs, lice, flies, disease, boils, hail, and locusts destroyed people, plants, and animals.
- A severe pestilence on the Egyptian livestock decimated their inventory of milk and meat.

The plagues God sent upon Egypt had a direct and immediate negative impact on its economy. More specifically, on Creation's ability to provide Pharaoh's kingdom with… food. How much this influenced his decision to set Israel free is up for discussion. However, had he not relented and brought a halt to the economic carnage, Egypt would have most certainly faced another famine, and this time there was no Joseph to rescue them.

Also, we cannot overlook the fact that food is central to the Passover celebration. All the food and every item on the table are used to retell the story of slavery and freedom. The Seder Plate holds the symbolic foods used during the telling. The meal is both solemn and joyful, and food is used to make the ancient story tangible, relevant, and memorable for each generation.

Then we turn to the book of Numbers. After God delivered the Israelites from Egypt, He told them that He was giving them what? "A land flowing with milk and honey." In essence, God's intention was to return them to a "garden" where He could re-establish His Covenant with them, giving them another chance to cultivate and keep Creation. When they rejected His offer, God placed them in a land that was anything *but* flowing with milk and honey. In fact, He did not give them an opportunity to cultivate and keep *any* garden. Instead, they had to rely on Him to provide mana for forty years.

In the books of Leviticus and Deuteronomy, we find the Mosaic Law included many feasts and festivals: Passover, the Feast of Unleavened Bread, the Feast of First Fruits, the Feast of Weeks, the Feast of Trumpets, and the Feast of Tabernacles. All these celebrations included abundant food. Each feast, in some way, reminded God's people that when they honored the Covenant to cultivate and keep creation, He would provide for them physically, emotionally, and spiritually. This is how He secured their identity as God's people, made in His image.

The remainder of Old Testament is filled with examples of how breaking the Covenant negatively impacted the nation of Israel for generations. Abraham and Lot divided their household because of a land dispute between their herdsmen. David went to war without God's permission and thus spilled innocent blood on the land. The consequences of both were enormous, and those are just two examples.

The New Testament arguably has more to say about the role food plays in the lives God's children than the Old Testament.

- The first people to whom God chose to reveal the birth of Jesus were the "lowly" shepherds. Even in Jesus' time, stewards of the land and Covenant keepers were taken for granted and devalued by society. God, however, highly valued them and rewarded them with a front-row seat to one of the most important events in human history.
- After Jesus was baptized, He went into the wilderness and fasted. He was hungry. So, what did Satan do? He went back to his Garden of Eden playbook and tried to get Jesus to undermine *His* relationship with the Father, Creation, and ultimately humanity, by accepting food.
- Throughout Jesus' ministry, food was the focal point of His lessons. He told us not to worry about obtaining it.[62] He created it in abundance, as

[62] Matthew 6:25

needed, to fulfill His mission in the moment.[63] He used the people's profound awareness of the importance of food to help them understand how important *He* is.[64]

- The most powerful use of food was toward the end of Jesus' ministry. He chose to spend the last evening prior to His death, doing what? Sharing a meal with those with whom He had formed His closest relationships. During that meal, He instituted the sacrament of communion that symbolically, yet directly, tied the consumption of something brought forth by Creation to His physical body and blood.

These are just a few examples that demonstrate how central food is in the story of God's Kingdom. However, it does not stop there. Consider your own life experiences. I am guessing that, like most people, you often share meals with those with whom you want to develop deeper relationships. It could be a potential spouse, a business relationship, or new friends at church.

Furthermore, when we practice hospitality, food is nearly always involved. I don't know about you, but my experience has been that the liveliest conversation, laughter, and relational connections happen around the table with the snacks. The spiritual dynamic is such that we naturally make generous micro-deposits of blessing into one another's lives.

---

[63] Matthew 14:13-21
[64] John 4:32-38, 6:27, 6:55

Additionally, I don't know of a situation where micro-deposits of blessing have a greater impact than when we share a meal with people who are suffering. There is a multiplier effect on identity building that is hard to describe. Walls that are normally difficult to scale come down. Spiritual doors that seemed previously to not exist open, especially for those who do not know Jesus. For them, the encounter can be so powerful that they exchange the lie for the truth and become builders of a Kingdom they did not even know existed.

There is more that I could say, but I think you get the point. Cultivating and keeping Creation is not about creating products for humanity to consume. It is the foundation of God's economic plan, and it is central to His strategy to secure human identity as bearers of His image. People are then unleashed to be fruitful, multiply, subdue the earth, and bring it into the domain of His Kingdom.

From a practical, real-world perspective, this means that creating robust local food networks—connecting farmers, processors, distributors, retailers, and consumers—is both a practical economic necessity and a covenantal act of restoration.

Economic cooperation will increase as followers of Jesus see it as God's remedy to end the theft of their resources by the spirits of control and competition.

In the coming years we will see followers of Jesus develop intentional cooperative relationships among businesses, churches, households, and organizations within a local community. They will likely include the following:

- Local citizens will take their monetary resources from traditional investments such as stocks and bonds and redirect that capital into collaborative community enterprises.
- Local exchange systems will be developed that enable value to circulate within the community without depending on the national monetary system.
- Local cooperative purchasing and resource acquisition arrangements will provide small businesses with a better value proposition.
- Producers of raw products will begin to add value by processing their products and selling locally vs. selling wholesale to large industrial processors.

The specific actions taken in each community may vary. However, the underlying principle is consistent: create value and retain it within the local community. This will reverse the trend of resources escaping the community on trading floors designed and managed by multinational corporations. Then those resources can be managed on local marketplace trading floors, retaining them within the Kingdom of God.

As it becomes evident that man's economic and monetary systems are no longer sustainable, the hunger for God's ways will grow, regardless of how "radical" they may seem.

God is opening the eyes of His children to "see" the identity theft that they and their loved ones have been subjected to on the trading floors designed and created by the kings of the earth. Books such as *The Revolt of the Public*, by Martin Gurri, *The Rise and Triumph of the Modern Self*, by Carl R. Trueman, and *The Unseen Realm*, by Dr. Michael Heiser (all of which are referenced in my books), have shifted the spiritual, cultural, and political narrative in favor of seeking what is real.

Followers of Jesus, who have never encountered a coherent, biblically grounded worldview for economic thought and action, are primed for something new. They are ready to reject the default assumption that economics is a technical discipline best left to experts.

A John 10:10 economic worldview, adopted as part of a broader educational ecosystem, will radically change how people interact with the world. They will participate faithfully in local economic restoration, seeing it as a natural pathway to the abundant life that Jesus came to give them, their family, and their neighbors.

I see this shift happening in real time. Today, when I talk to people who have recently read my books, concepts like trading floors, micro-deposits, and economic ecosystems do not sound as radical to them as they did to readers in early 2021 when I first released *I Came to Give*. This tells me that *God is moving*.

In Conclusion

What lies ahead is the hard but rewarding process of breaking the spiritual inertia behind our embrace of today's "economic traditions of men." Beliefs, habits, and the defense of existing systems have been pressed into the church for centuries through a false dilemma. The good news is—and history confirms—God's principles and ways are real. They are the "third option" that He has always offered humanity. Today He stands ready to work with you to restore them within the jurisdiction He has given to you. That leaves each of us with two very important questions:

- Are we ready, individually and collectively, to take God at His word and restore His way of creating, stewarding, and deploying His resources during this critical time in history?
- Do we have the courage to engage in an area where the church has not meaningfully confronted the enemy for centuries?

There is no escaping the reality that indeed, the enemy is a thief, and he came to steal, kill, and destroy every resource God has entrusted to us. Yet Jesus came to give us another option. Another way. Another life. One filled with His definition of abundance.

My prayer is that those who "see" the reality of the John 10:10 economic worldview can no longer "unsee" it. This will leave them with no choice as they realize that governments and financial institutions cannot fix what is broken. The body of Christ, empowered by the Spirit and equipped with the principles of the Kingdom—can.

Followers of Jesus will be moved to act, not by coercion, but by a Holy Spirit empowered love for their families and their neighbors to be set free from bondage of the economic traditions of men. In response, they will engage in patient, persistent, love-fueled action in their homes, churches, and communities, one trading floor and one micro-deposit at a time.

As more of God's people participate, the truth of Jesus' abundant life will become undeniably visible and compelling. The contrast with Satan's fragile, scarcity-driven, theft-resourced lie will become a powerful evangelistic witness. It will lead countless beloved image bearers to exchange the lie for the truth and worship the Creator who designed it for us all… in the beginning.

God is inviting every follower of Jesus to join Him in this Great Restoration. To begin, you can learn more by digging into the "meat" behind this book. Or, if you are ready to get started transforming the economy of your household, church, community or nation into what God originally intended, visit https://regeneco.org. We stand ready to serve you in whatever way God leads.

May the Lord bless you with His abundant life!

Acknowledgments

To my family… When *I Came to Give* was released in 2021, we all sensed that God was up to something significant. Through the years leading up to its release, and since, you've supported me with your encouragement, trust, and patience. I believe God is saying, it's "go time." Whatever that looks like in the coming years, this has been for you—my wife, children, and grandchildren—both born and yet to come. May God's Kingdom become more manifest on earth each passing year and may you all be blessed with *His* abundant life.

To the countless friends and co-laborers in the Kingdom that God has blessed me with over the last twenty-five years. I love you all. It's time to get busy working together to fulfill God's mandate and complete His Grand Building Project.

To my Lord, Savior, and *King*—Jesus. You, Father, and Holy Spirit are on the move in ways that are increasingly obvious to the world. May your followers put on their identity as your brethren and heirs to the Kingdom and get to the blessed work of answering your prayer for it to come to earth as it is in heaven.

$10.99
ISBN 978-1-7357090-9-3
51099>
9 781735 709093

www.ingramcontent.com/pod-product-compliance
Lightning Source LLC
LaVergne TN
LVHW022109200926
848481LV00003B/1129